Face-to-Face INSECTS

P9-DZX-714

What's Inside?

THIS WAY TO FOOD

Insect World

Insects live almost everywhere. You can find them in your backyard as well as on the highest mountaintops and in the driest deserts. It's easy to spot an insect. It always has six legs. Most insects have wings, too. On this page, there are a few amazing insects for you to get to know!

Cicadas are the world's loudest insects. They live in fields, forests, and deserts.

This rain forest stick insect is the world's longest insect.

A dragonfly lives near ponds. In short bursts, it flies faster than most other insects.

WOW!
Scientists have named over one million kinds of insects. But there may still be millions more to find!

The world's heaviest insect is probably the Goliath beetle. It lives in the rain forest.

Bee

Many kinds of bees live together in nests, or in hives built for them by people. In the summer, bees fly from flower to flower to suck up a sweet juice, called nectar. They take this juice back to the nest and turn it into honey to eat. Bees also use a sticky yellow flower dust, called pollen, for food.

Q Why do bees make honey?

A In the winter, flowers die, so honeybees can't collect nectar anymore. Luckily, they still have a store of delicious honey left over from the summer for them to eat.

Ahh! Breakfast!

HONEY

✳ A bumblebee has its own shopping baskets to carry its food! There are hairy containers on the bee's back legs that the bee fills with pollen to take home.

✳ When a honeybee finds a tasty supply of food, it flies back to the hive and does a special wiggly dance to show its nest-mates the way to the food!

THIS WAY TO FOOD

✳ Flowers don't stand a chance against a carpenter bee. This crafty insect saws a hole in a flower with its sharp jaws to reach the sweet nectar inside.

It's a Laugh!
Where did the bee wait for the bus?
At the buzz stop!

Feeding Frenzy

When it comes to finding food, insects are at the head of the class! They have sharp eyesight and two long feelers, called antennae, to help them smell and feel for snacks. Many insects munch on leaves or drink juice from flowers. Others are fierce meat eaters that eat other creepy-crawlers.

▷ Gotcha!

A praying mantis is a deadly hunter. It sits on a leaf and waits for a fly. Suddenly, it stretches out its spiny front legs and grabs its snack!

WOW! A human flea has a tiny appetite. It can go for nearly four months without a single meal!

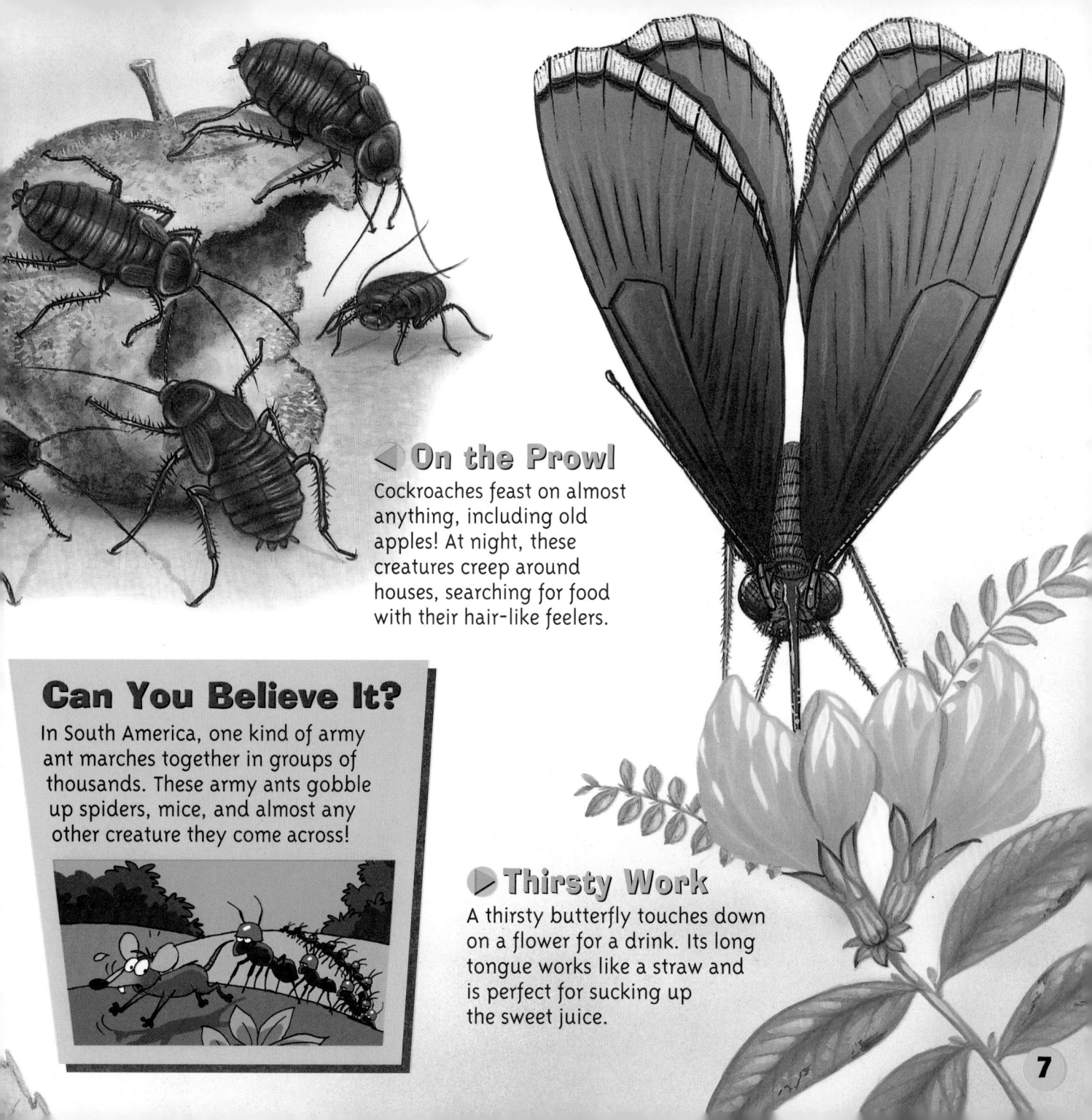

On the Prowl

Cockroaches feast on almost anything, including old apples! At night, these creatures creep around houses, searching for food with their hair-like feelers.

Can You Believe It?

In South America, one kind of army ant marches together in groups of thousands. These army ants gobble up spiders, mice, and almost any other creature they come across!

Thirsty Work

A thirsty butterfly touches down on a flower for a drink. Its long tongue works like a straw and is perfect for sucking up the sweet juice.

Cricket

Crickets are champion jumpers! They have superstrong back legs that help them leap high into the air. This chirping insect usually comes out at night, when it searches for food. By day, it hides under rocks or in shallow holes in the ground. If it is lucky, it finds plenty of plants and even other insects to eat.

It's a Laugh!
What do you get if you cross an insect with a rabbit?
Bugs Bunny!

❈ Like you, a cricket has its eyes and mouth on its head. But if you want to find its ears, you need to look on its front legs!

❈ A romantic male cricket will sing to attract a female mate. He sings his love song by rubbing his wings together.

Q Why do crickets lose their skin?

A When a cricket grows, its skin does not grow with it. Instead, the cricket sheds its old skin and grows a new skin underneath. It then eats the old skin for breakfast!

Mmm, tasty!

❈ Hungry predators know to stay away from a South African bush cricket. This fierce-looking insect is covered in a spiky suit of armor. It also tastes disgusting!

On the Move

The countryside is full of roaming insects both day and night. On the ground, beetles scurry around on their short legs while grasshoppers and crickets hop through the grass. Up above, all kinds of winged fliers whiz around. You can even find insects swimming in ponds and streams.

Can You Believe It?

A flea can jump up to 100 times its own height. If you could jump like that, you'd be able to leap to the top of a 25-story building!

Do the Backstroke!

A back swimmer lives in a pond. It swims on its back and rows with its back legs. It looks just like it is rowing a boat!

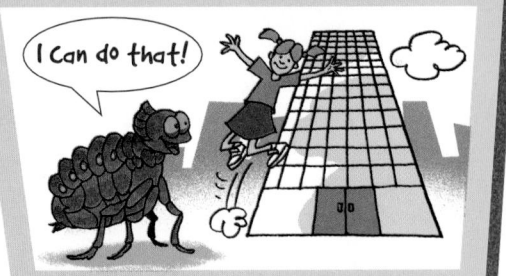

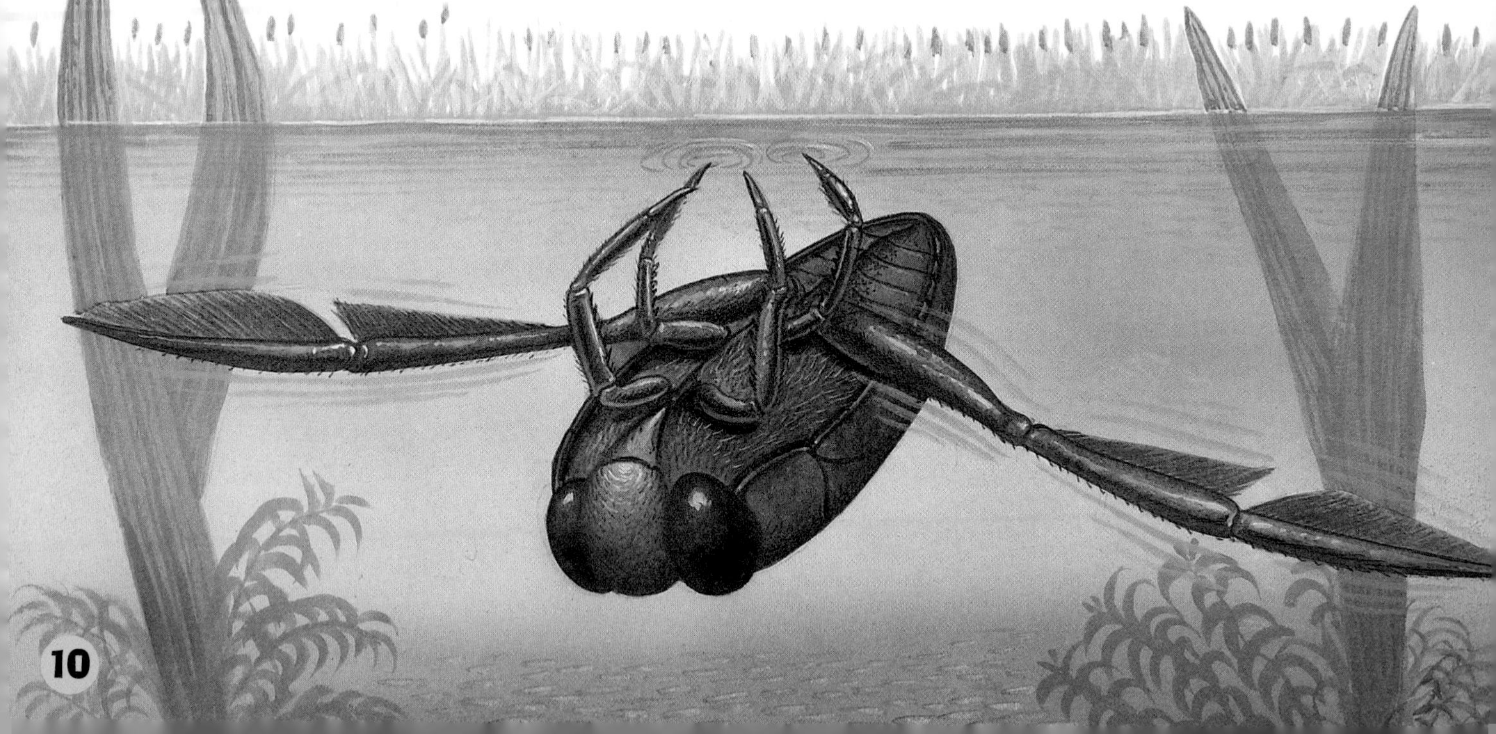

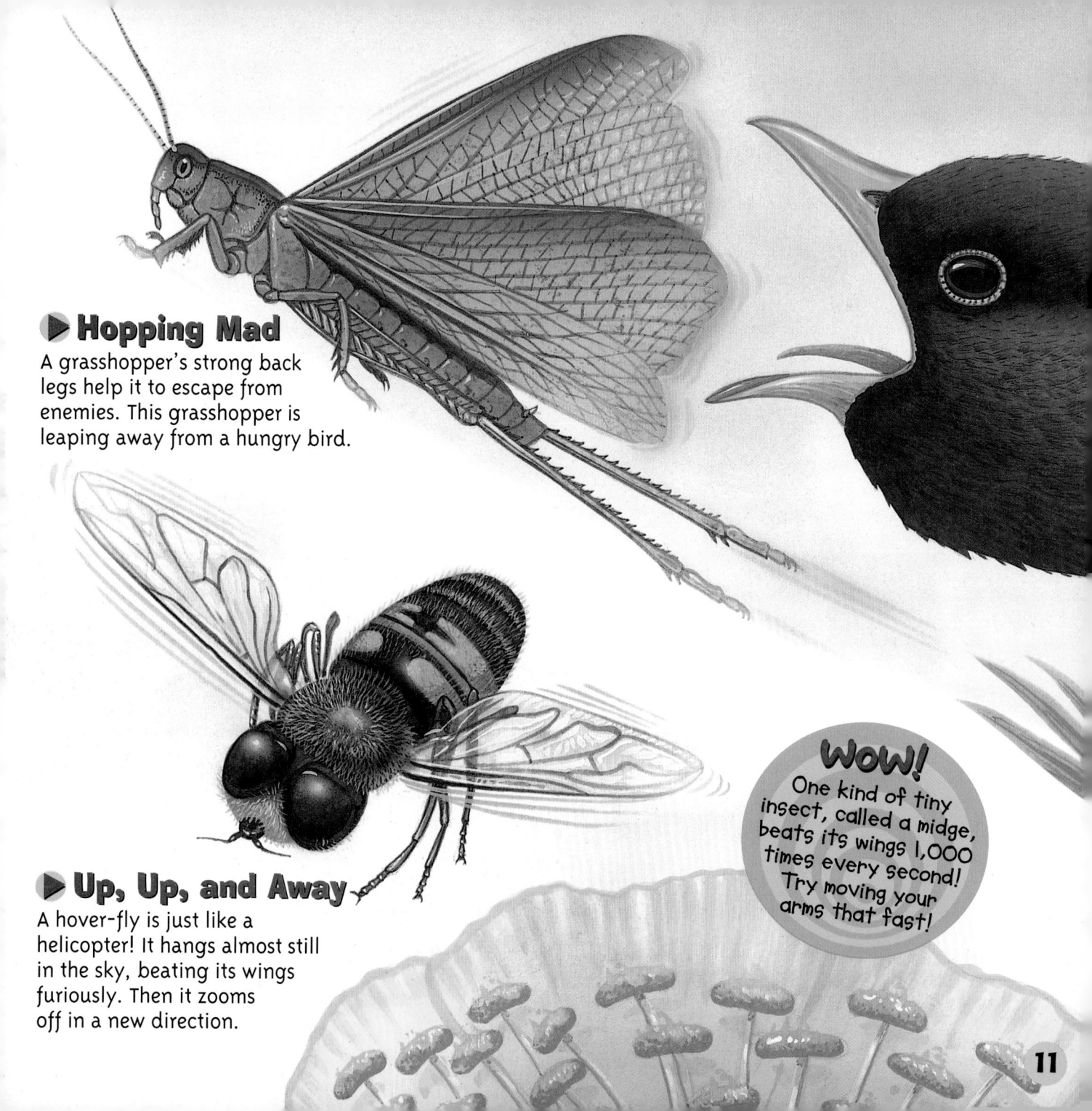

▶ Hopping Mad

A grasshopper's strong back legs help it to escape from enemies. This grasshopper is leaping away from a hungry bird.

▶ Up, Up, and Away

A hover-fly is just like a helicopter! It hangs almost still in the sky, beating its wings furiously. Then it zooms off in a new direction.

WOW!

One kind of tiny insect, called a midge, beats its wings 1,000 times every second! Try moving your arms that fast!

11

Beetle

Beetles come in all shapes, sizes, and colors. A few, such as this palm beetle, have brightly patterned bodies. Beetles spend most of the time crawling around, but they can fly, too. When a beetle is on the ground, it protects its wings under tough covers called wing cases.

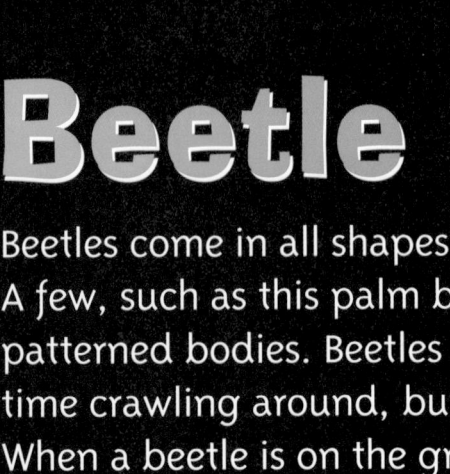

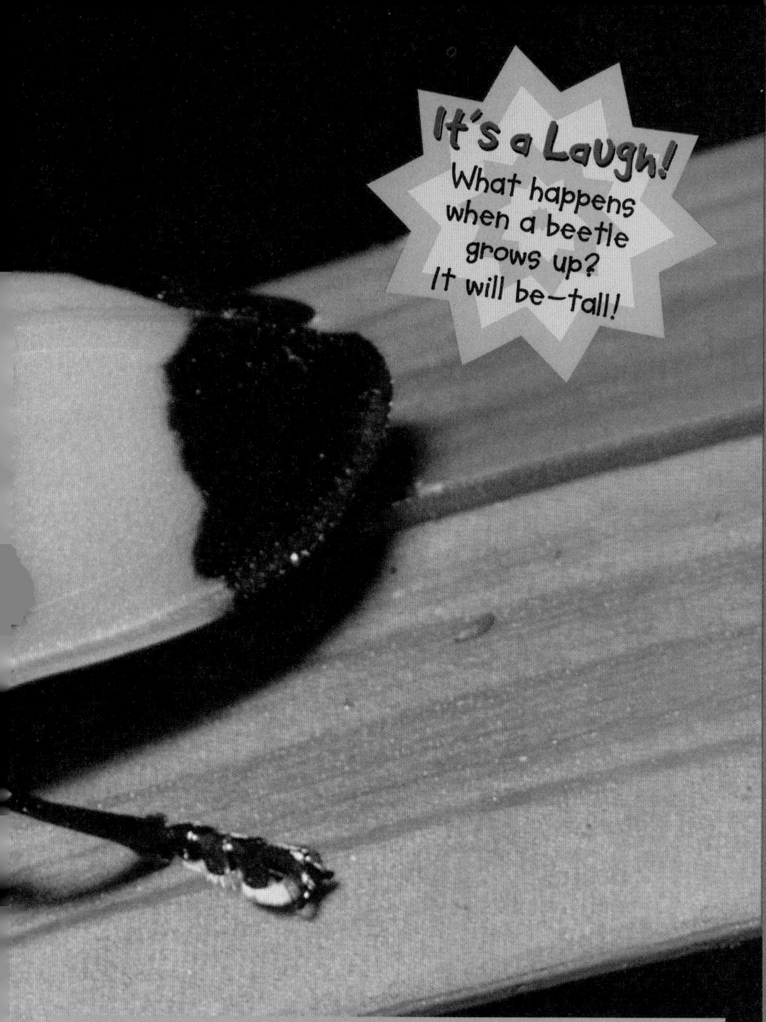

A darkling beetle stands on its head to drink! Early in the morning, in the desert, it waits for dew to form on its back. Then the beetle tips its head forward until the dew rolls into its mouth!

Male stag beetles enjoy a good fight. One beetle grabs hold of the other one with its huge pincerlike jaws and tries to push it over.

Most beetles don't take care of their babies, but some fungus beetles are attentive moms. They look after their baby grubs until the grubs are fully grown.

Q Are beetles strong?

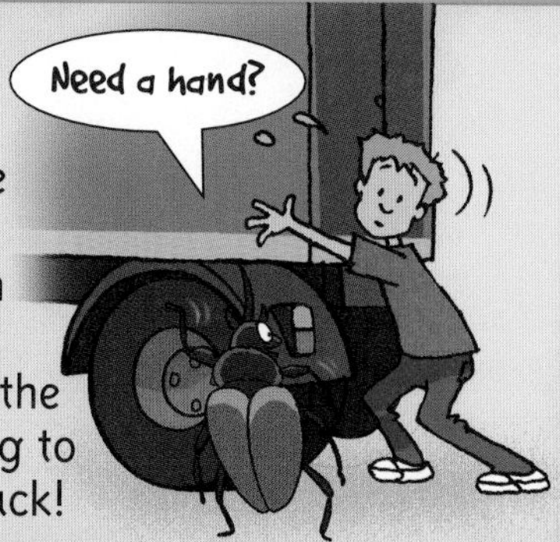

A Yes. Beetles are incredibly strong! A rhinoceros beetle can carry objects that are more than 850 times heavier than itself. That's the same as you trying to lift up a heavy truck!

Need a hand?

Home, Sweet Home

Insects live in all kinds of different homes. Some insects just take a nap under a handy leaf or stone, out of sight of prowling enemies. Others build their own homes. Wasps and termites work in large teams and make truly amazing places to live!

▼ Busy Builders

Tiny termites build enormous towers out of mud and wood. Underneath each one is an underground nest full of tunnels where the termites live. On the right, you can see inside a termite's nest. Take a look below to see a close-up of the busy builder!

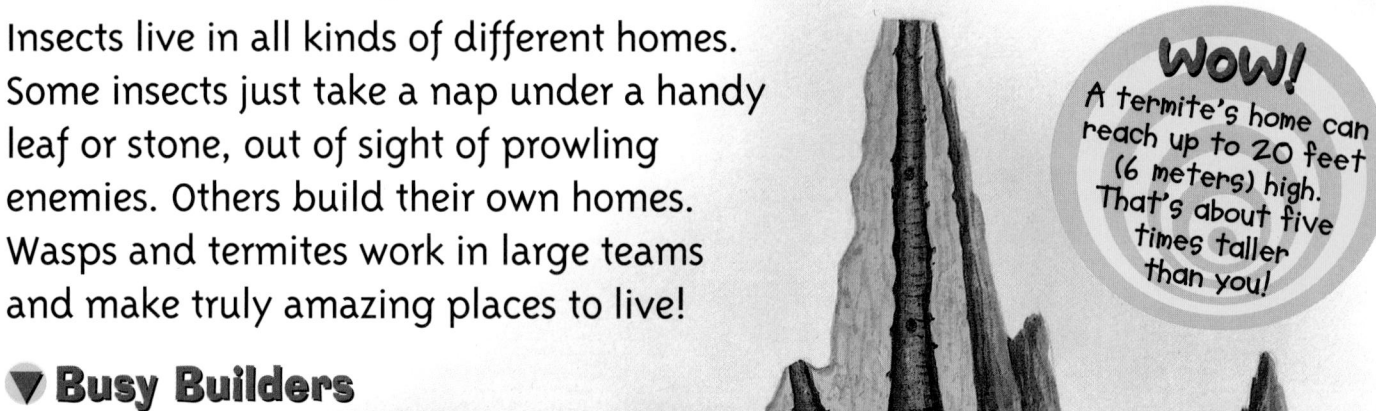

WOW! A termite's home can reach up to 20 feet (6 meters) high. That's about five times taller than you!

▲ Weird Wallpaper

Many wasps make their nests by chewing up plants and wood, then turning them into mushy paper. They use the paper to build the walls for their home.

Can You Believe It?

A few insects live on other animals! Some rain forest moths make their homes in the shaggy fur of a creature called a sloth. They hitch a ride as the sloth moves slowly along.

Can you speed up a little?

▼ Mobile Home

A young caddis fly lives in a pond. It builds its tubelike home from twigs and tiny stones. When the creature is on the move, it takes its home along, too.

Dragonfly

Have you ever seen a dragonfly darting across a river or a pond? In the air, this large, brightly colored insect is an amazing acrobat. It can even fly backward! Buzzing mosquitoes and flies are no match for this lightning-quick hunter with its enormous eyes.

It's a Laugh!

Which insect lives in an office?
A computer bug!

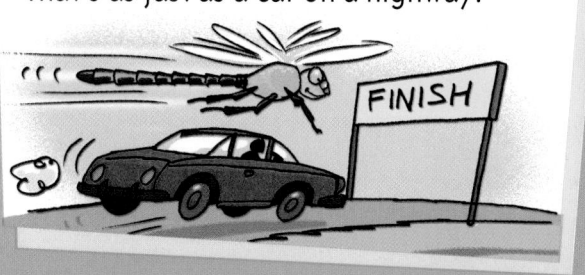

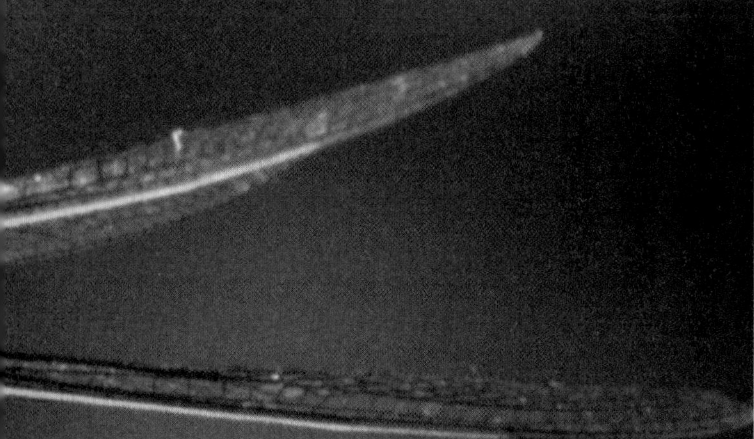

Can a dragonfly walk?

A No! Even though a dragonfly has six legs, it can't walk. However, its legs are useful for catching food and perching on twigs.

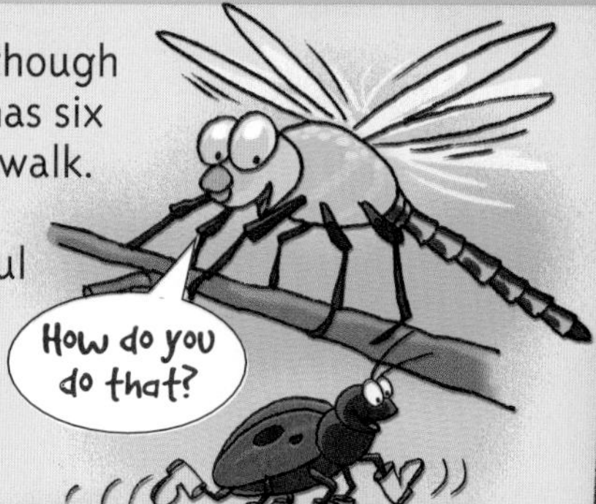
How do you do that?

A dragonfly catches its dinner in midair. As it flies, it holds its spiny legs together to make a tiny basket. Tasty insects fall into the basket and are trapped.

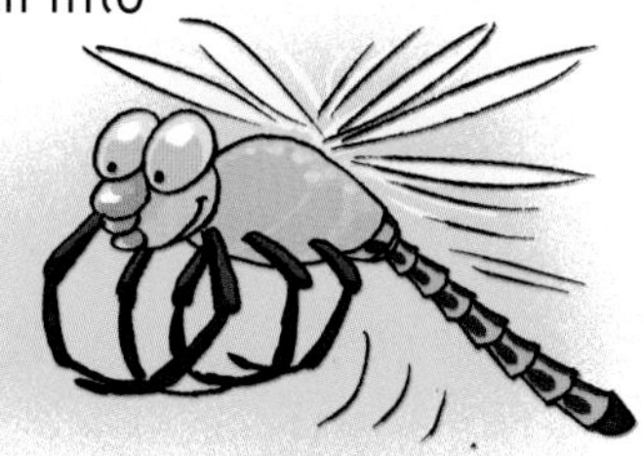

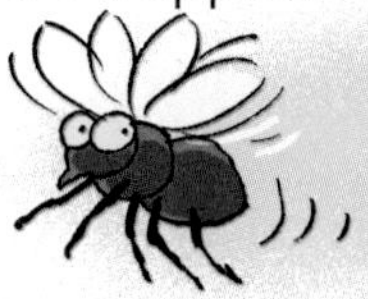

A dragonfly is one of the speediest insects around. It can zoom along at up to 59 miles (94 kilometers) per hour. That's as fast as a car on a highway!

FINISH

A young dragonfly is called a nymph. It lives completely underwater, grabbing fish, tadpoles, and other treats for its dinner.

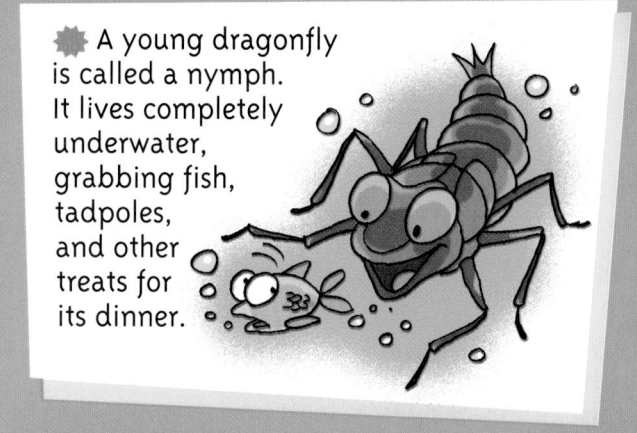

Staying Alive

Animals are always on the lookout for a tasty insect snack, so creepy-crawlers need to watch out! Many insects hide or stay very still so that their enemies don't notice them. Other minibeasts have hidden weapons for frightening off attackers.

▶ Armed and Dangerous

A bombardier beetle is like a tiny kettle. When an enemy approaches, it boils chemicals inside its body, then lets out a scalding gas with a loud pop. Ouch!

18

◀ Warning Colors

This moth caterpillar is brightly colored with poisonous spikes to keep it safe from harm. Bright colors are a way of saying, "Don't eat me. I taste terrible!"

WOW!
One kind of moth caterpillar avoids being noticed by looking like a bird dropping on a leaf!

▶ A Clever Disguise

Take a look at these rose thorns. Now look closer: One of them is a thorn bug! This spiky insect fools its enemies by pretending to be a thorn on a plant.

3 Soon, the caterpillar eats so much that its skin splits! But don't worry, there's a new skin underneath. This happens several times, until the caterpillar grows big and strong.

Time for a change of skin!

You're weird!

4 After a few weeks, the caterpillar is fully grown. It then turns into a pupa, which has a hard case around its body. Some insects stay like this for months!

What is that?

No idea. But it's been here forever!

5 Inside the case, strange things are happening. The insect is slowly changing form! Then one day, the case splits and a butterfly pushes its way out.

Eek! Look at that!

I knew something was going on!

6 At first, the butterfly's wings are soft and crumpled. But after a few hours, they harden and stretch out. The butterfly flutters its colorful wings and off it flies!

Phew! I've had enough of those ladybugs!

Puzzle Time

Here are a few puzzles to try. You can look back in the book to help you find the answers.

True or False?

How much do you know about insects? Answer these true or false questions to find out.

1 Bumblebees carry nectar in pouches on the backs of their legs. Hint: Go to page 5.

2 Crickets have ears just behind their eyes. Hint: Go to page 9.

3 A darkling beetle drinks rain during storms. Hint: Go to page 13.

4 Young dragonflies live underwater. Hint: Go to page 17.

What's for Breakfast?

These insects are hungry. Can you help them find their food?

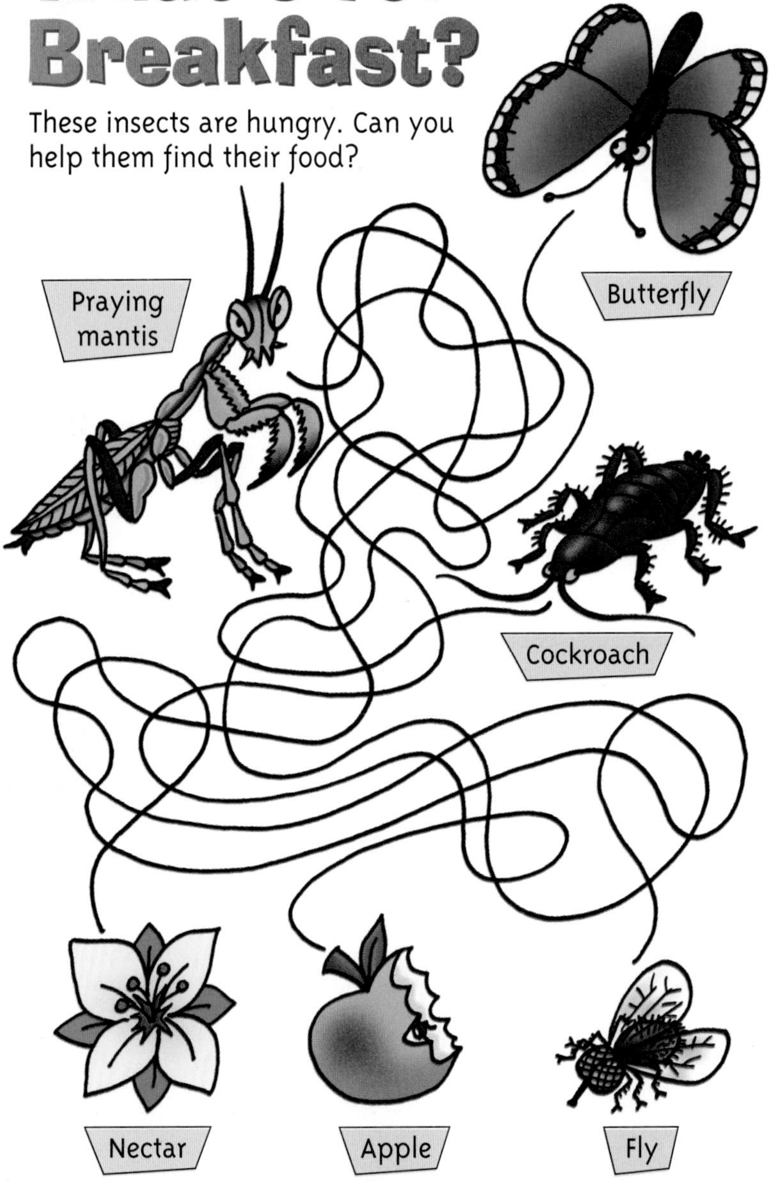

Butterfly

Praying mantis

Cockroach

Nectar

Apple

Fly

Close-up

We've zoomed in on these insects. Can you tell which insects they are?

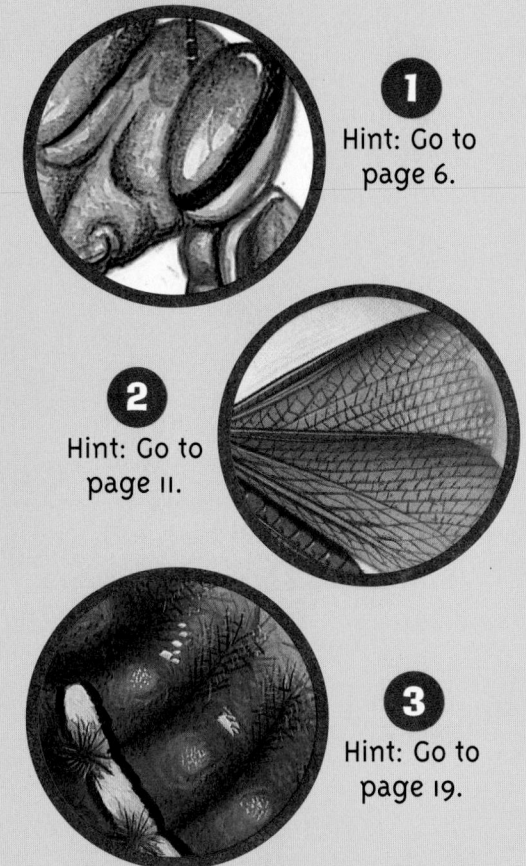

1 Hint: Go to page 6.

2 Hint: Go to page 11.

3 Hint: Go to page 19.

Index

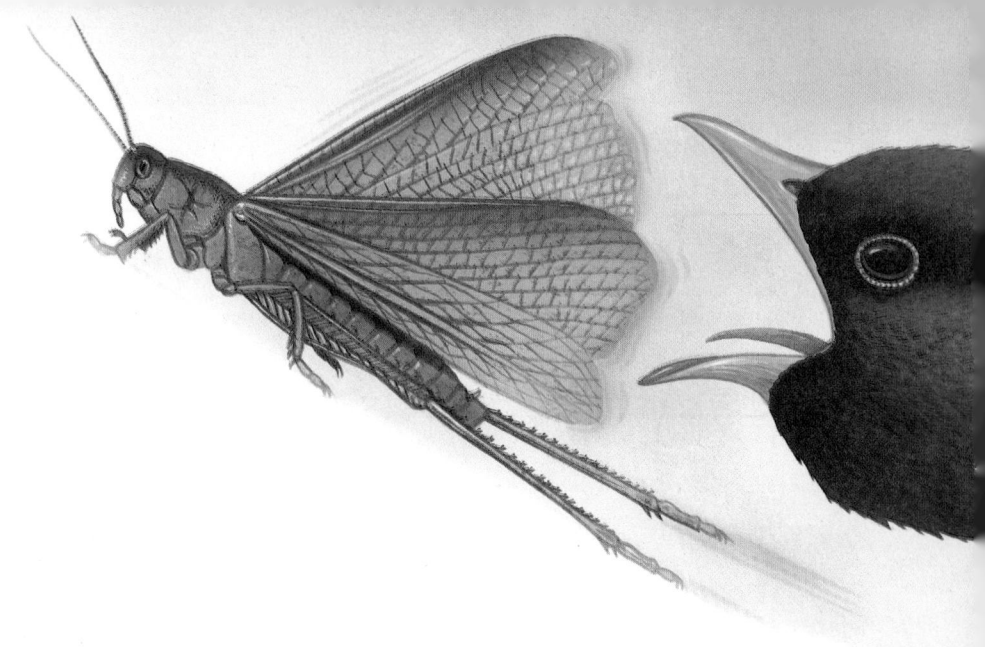

Created by act-two for Scholastic Inc.
Copyright © act-two, 2001.
All rights reserved. Published by Scholastic Inc.
SCHOLASTIC and associated logos are trademarks
and/or registered trademarks of Scholastic Inc.

Main illustrations: Alan Male
Cartoon illustrations: Simon Clare
except for pp. 20–21 Geo Parkin, p. 23 Alan Rowe
Consultant: Barbara Taylor
Photographs: Cover image of assassin bug OSF/David M.
Dennis, pp. 4–5 NHPA/Stephen Dalton,
pp. 8–9 Panda/V. Giannotti/FLPA;
pp. 12–13 Michael and Patricia Fogden,
pp. 16–17 NHPA /Stephen Dalton

ISBN 0-439-31713-4

12 11 10 9 8 7 6 5 4 3   1 2 3 4 5 6/0

Printed in the U.S.A.

First Scholastic printing, November 2001